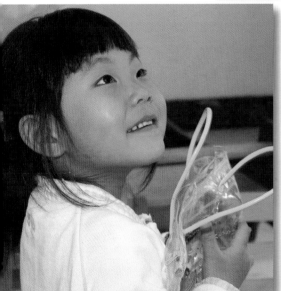

Kindergarten Day
China and USA

A Flip-Me-Over Book

Trish Marx and Ellen B. Senisi

A GLOBAL FUND FOR
Children
BOOK

ichi Charlesbridge

Come in! It's time for kindergarten to start.

Our *lǎo shī,* or teacher, gives us a big hug. "Let's quiet down," she says, "so we can start our first lesson."

老师 *lǎo shī:* teacher

Chinese can also be written in *pinyin* by using the English alphabet to help people sound out the characters. Mandarin Chinese is a tonal language in which the rising and falling tones of each syllable indicate different meanings. *Pinyin* uses four accent marks to show these different tones; for example, *Mā* (mother), *Má* (linen), *Mǎ* (horse), *Mà* (to scold). When you see a *pinyin* word in this book, use the spelling to help you sound it out. Then try it out on a friend!

9:00 a.m. China

9:00 p.m. USA

Our fairy-tale book is written in Chinese characters. Some of them look like a little picture. This is the character for *sēn lín,* or "forest."

森林

Do you see the trees?

Lǎo shī also reads to us in English.

We say the letters of each word.

C-O-Y-O-T-E. Coyote.

That's a fun word to say.

森林 *sēn lín:* forest.

10:00 a.m. China

10:00 p.m. USA

It's time for *měi shù,* or art class.
"Gather your colored pencils, crayons,
and paper," *lǎo shī* says.

Sometimes we draw by ourselves.
Then we paint or color our pictures.
Other times we draw together. We hang
our finished pictures in the classroom.

美术 *měi shù:* art class

11:00 a.m. China

11:00 p.m. USA

"It's time to eat," *lǎo shī* says, as she prepares our *wǔ cān,* or lunch.

We pick up the vegetables and rice with our chopsticks. We sip the soup from the bowl. When we finish our meal, we help our *lǎo shī* clear the table.

午餐 *wǔ cān:* lunch

12:00 noon China

12:00 midnight USA

Surprise!

"It's someone's *shēng rì,*" *lǎo shī* says. "Tell us what you will learn to do, now that you are one year older."

That makes us all think about what we want to do—read longer words, ride a bicycle, tie our shoes.

We sing "Happy Birthday." Then it's time for cake!

生 日 *shēng rì:* birthday

12:30 p.m. China
12:30 a.m. USA

At recess the jungle gym is where we *wán,* or play. We are fishermen in sampans, sailing the sea. We are explorers, climbing a mountain. We are emperors on golden thrones.

We run and jump and kick and dance around our playground.

玩 *wán:* play

1:00 p.m. China

1:00 a.m. USA

When we play with our toys, *lǎo shī* asks us to *fēn xiǎng,* or share. Sometimes this is hard to do.

"Tell me what the problem is," *lǎo shī* says. We each take a turn explaining how we feel. When we're done, *lǎo shī* talks quietly with us. He helps us understand what sharing really is.

分享 *fēn xiǎng:* share

2:00 p.m. China

2:00 a.m. USA

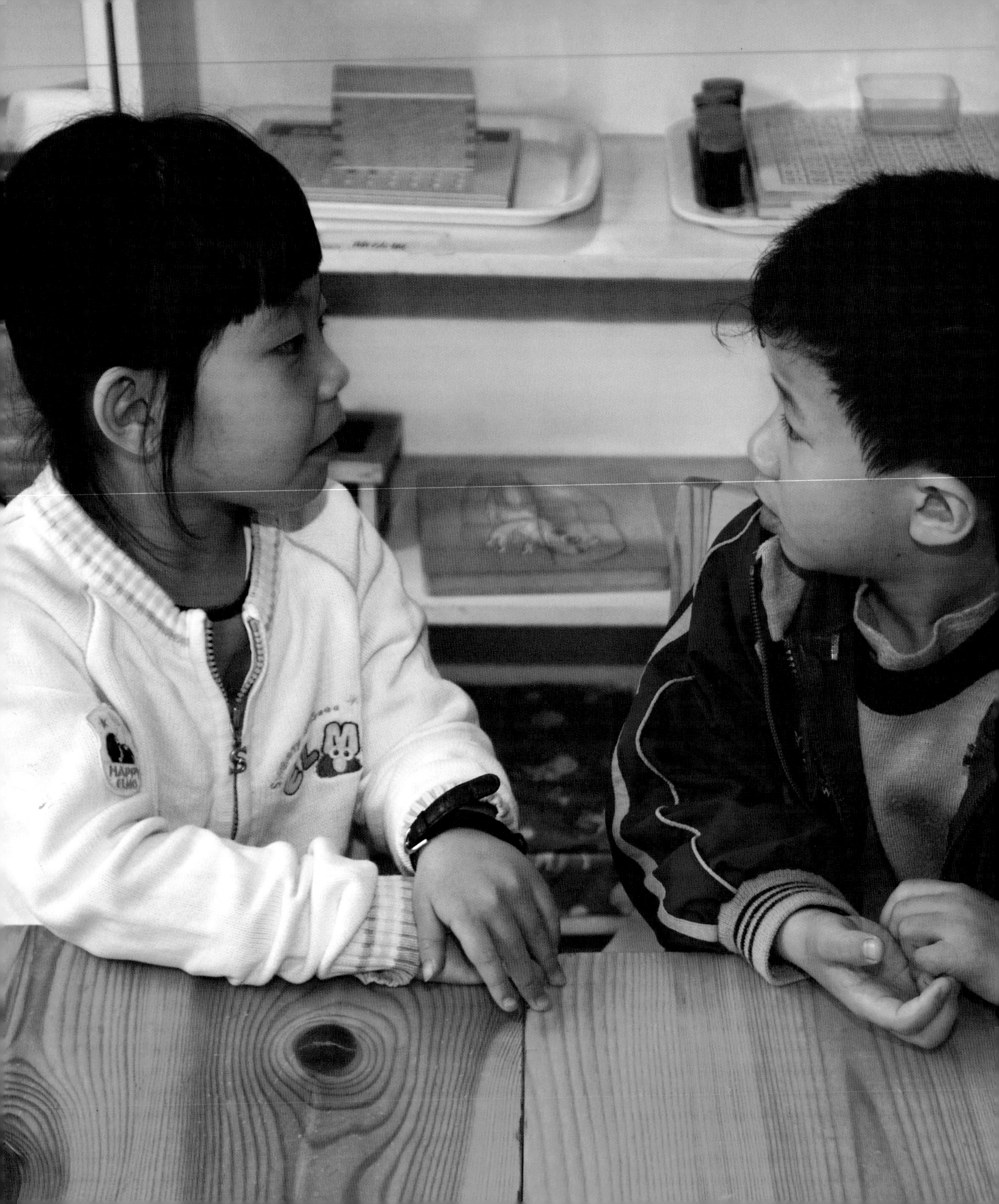

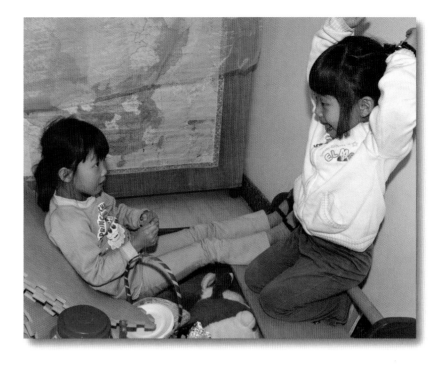

We take time to talk with our *péng yǒu,* or friends. Sometimes we share what's in our hearts. Other times we tell a funny story. Sometimes we just surprise our friends: "I'm glad you're my friend," we say.

朋友 *péng yǒu:* friends

2:30 p.m. China

2:30 a.m. USA

Want to go to the USA?
Flip me over and
start again.

Kindergarten Day
USA and China
A Flip-Me-Over Book

Trish Marx and Ellen B. Senisi

Yī, èr, sān, sì, wǔ. Fingers help us count . . . our books, our crayons, our friends.

If we had lots of fingers, we could count the miles across the ocean to the United States. We wonder if children there count things, too. Do they wonder about us?

一 *yī*, 二 *èr*, 三 *sān*, 四 *sì*, 五 *wǔ:*
one, two, three, four, five

3:00 p.m. China

3:00 a.m. USA

We practice telling time on a clock. The little hand shows the hour. The big hand shows the minute. "It's 3:00 in the afternoon here," our teacher says, "but in China it's 3:00 in the morning." We wonder if the children in China are sleeping right now. Do they ever wonder what we are doing?

3:00 p.m. USA

3:00 a.m. China

We take a break and huddle with our friends. We make up games or just hang out together. We are learning how to make friends, how to laugh with friends, and how to BE a friend.

2:30 p.m. USA

2:30 a.m. China

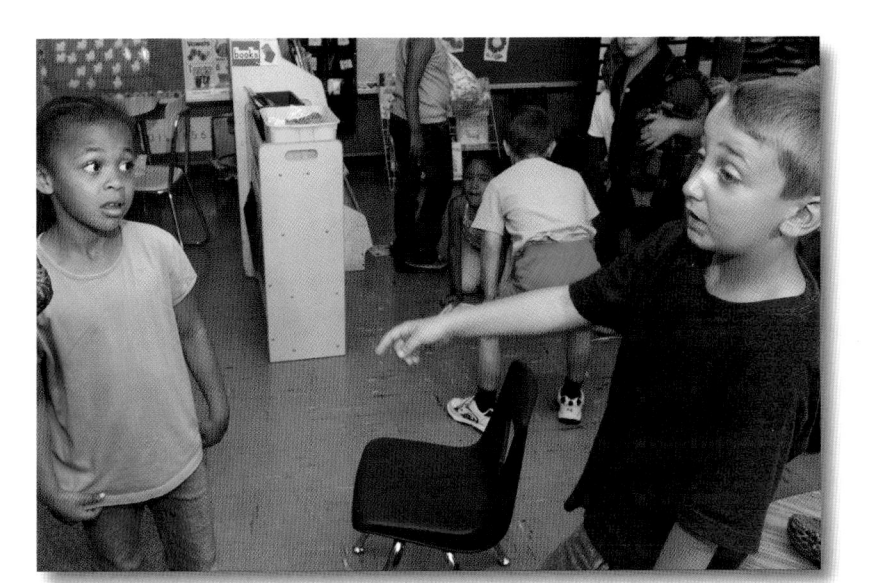

One of our kindergarten rules is
Always use your soft voice indoors.

Sometimes when something upsets us,
we forget this rule and raise our voices.
No matter what problem we have, our
teacher helps us feel better.

2:00 p.m. USA

2:00 a.m. China

"Let's climb the monkey bars!"

"Catch that ball!"

It's recess. We can use our loud voices
and run and play when we're outside.
Our teacher says that we're letting
off steam.

1:00 p.m. USA

1:00 a.m. China

"It's your special day," our teacher says to the birthday boy. We sing birthday wishes. The birthday boy passes out cupcakes. "Thank you," we say.

Then everything is quiet except for the munch, munch, munch as we eat our cupcakes.

12:30 p.m. USA

12:30 a.m. China

When the lunch bell rings, we put away our markers and crayons.

When we get to the lunchroom, we wait in line. The lunchroom worker says, "Eat your carrots."

Working hard all morning makes us hungry.

12:00 noon USA

12:00 midnight China

We draw pictures for our families. Our can of crayons has every color!

On sunny days we go outside. We can draw whatever is around us—a tiny ant, a blade of grass, or a big tree.

11:00 a.m. USA

11:00 p.m. China

First we sing our ABCs. A is for "apple" and "animal"!

Then we put the letters together and sound them out. C-R-O-C-O-D-I-L-E. Crocodile. Words!

We know enough words to read some books. The best part is reading with our friends.

10:00 a.m. USA

10:00 p.m. China

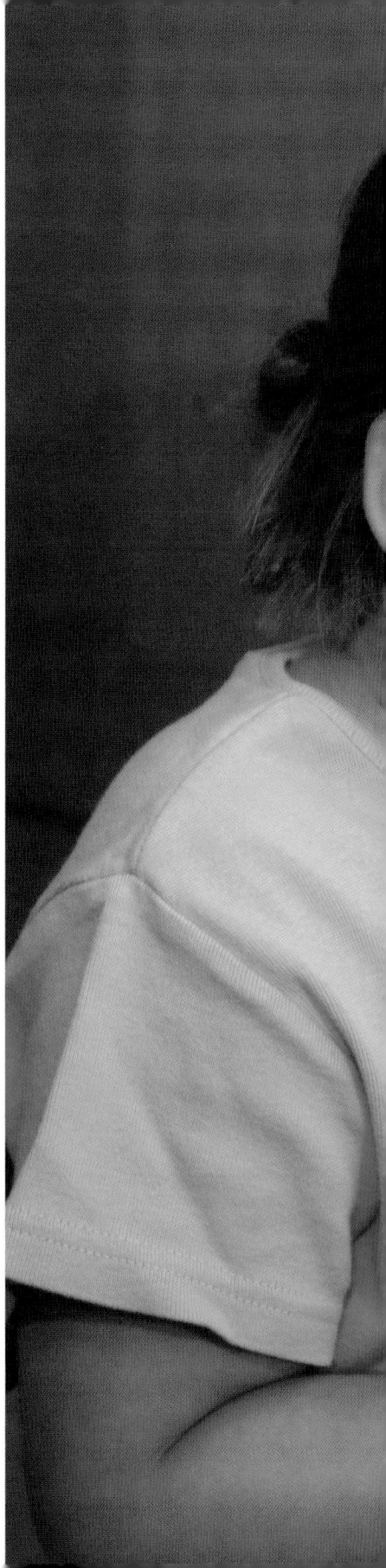

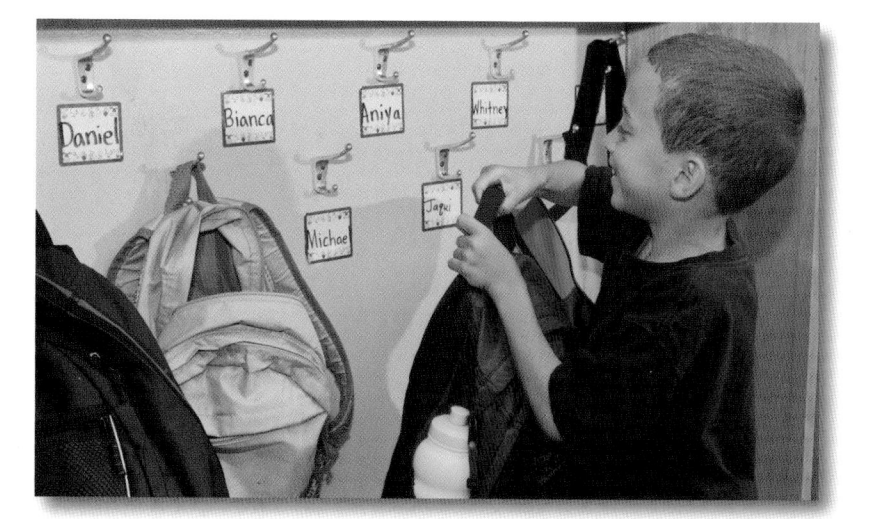

Come in! It's time for kindergarten to start.

Our teachers greet us at the door. "Good morning. How are you?" they say. Then we find our friends and say "good morning" to them, too.

There are twenty-four hours in each day. The clock's little hand shows what hour it is. Its big hand shows the minutes. When you see the letters a.m. after the time, it means "before noon." The letters p.m. mean "after noon." From March to November most of the people in the United States turn their clocks forward by an hour to conserve energy. During these months, whatever time it is in the school in Schenectady, it is twelve hours later in the school in Beijing.

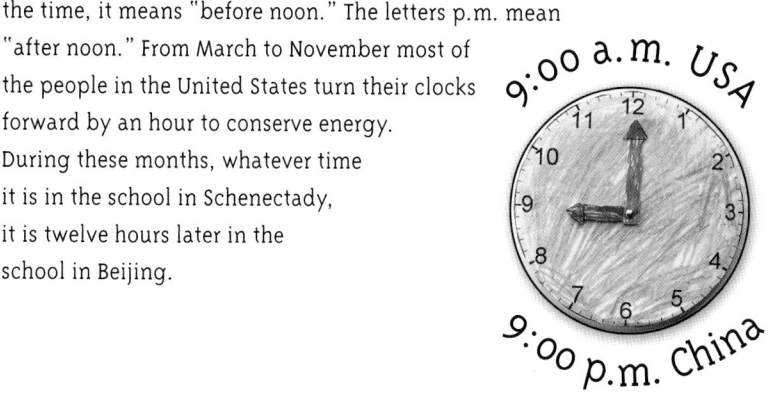

There is an old saying in the United States of America, "If you dig a hole deep enough, you'll reach China." That is because the People's Republic of China is about halfway around the world from the United States of America. When the stars are out in the United States, the sun is shining in China. When you are at school in the United States, the children in China are asleep. When you are asleep, the children in China are at school!

Turn the page to visit a class in Schenectady, New York. Then flip the book upside down to join a class in Beijing, China.

Welcome to kindergarten! *Huān yíng guāng lín yòu ér yuán!*

For Annie, with love—T. M.
For my favorite teachers: my mom and dad—E. B. S.

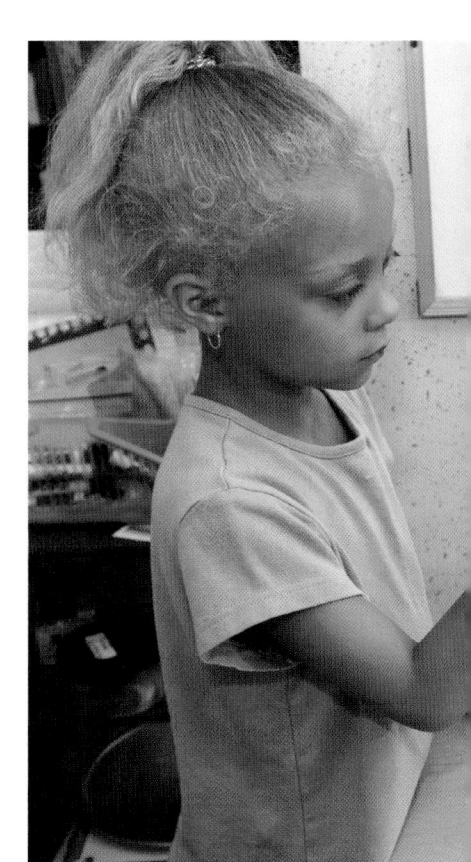

ACKNOWLEDGMENTS

Thanks to kindergarteners and staff at Zoller Elementary School in Schenectady, New York, and at Little Oak Children's House in Beijing, China. A special thanks to Dr. Janet Gulden, Magnet Coordinator, and Jon Pan, Mandarin Chinese instructor at Diamond Path Elementary School of International Studies, Minnesota.

The Global Fund for Children, which helped to develop this book, is a nonprofit organization committed to advancing the dignity of children and youth around the world. Global Fund for Children Books teach young people to value diversity and help them become productive and caring citizens of the world.

Part of the proceeds from this book's sales will be donated to The Global Fund for Children to support innovative community-based organizations that serve the world's most vulnerable children and youth. Details about the donation of royalties can be obtained by writing to Charlesbridge Publishing and The Global Fund for Children.

The Global Fund for Children
1101 Fourteenth Street NW, Suite 420
Washington, DC 20005
(202) 331-9003
www.globalfundforchildren.org

Published by Charlesbridge
85 Main Street
Watertown, MA 02472
(617) 926-0329
www.charlesbridge.com

Library of Congress Cataloging-in-Publication Data
Marx, Trish.
    Kindergarten day USA and China / Kindergarten Day China and USA / Trish Marx and Ellen B. Senisi.
        p. cm.
    ISBN 978-1-58089-219-3 (reinforced for library use)
    ISBN 978-1-58089-220-9 (softcover)
1. Kindergarten—United States—Juvenile literature. 2.Kindergarten—China—Juvenile literature.
I. Senisi, Ellen B. II. Title.
LB1205.M37 2010
372.21'80973—dc22   2009026881

Printed in China
(hc) 10 9 8 7 6 5 4 3 2 1
(sc) 10 9 8 7 6 5 4 3 2 1

Display type and text type set in Chaloops and Triplex
Color separations by Chroma Graphics, Singapore
Printed and bound February 2010 by Yangjiang Millenium Litho Ltd. in Yangjiang, Guangdong, China
Production supervision by Brian G. Walker
Designed by Susan Mallory Sherman

Kindergarten Day USA and China

A Flip-Me-Over Book

Trish Marx and Ellen B. Senisi

A GLOBAL FUND FOR

Children

BOOK

Charlesbridge

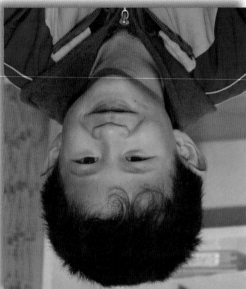

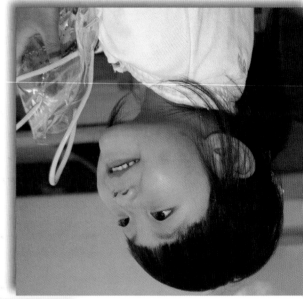